Research Activities of the
Department of Transportation:
A Report to Congress

U.S. Department of Transportation

Research and Innovative Technology Administration

March 2005

ACRONYMS

BTS	Bureau of Transportation Statistics
DHS	Department of Homeland Security
DOC	Department of Commerce
DOD	Department of Defense
DOE	Department of Energy
DOT	Department of Transportation
FAA	Federal Aviation Administration
FHWA	Federal Highway Administration
FMCSA	Federal Motor Carrier Safety Administration
FRA	Federal Railroad Administration
FTA	Federal Transit Administration
FY	Fiscal Year
GWU	George Washington University
HFCC	Human Factors Coordinating Committee
ITS	Intelligent Transportation Systems
JPDO	Joint Planning and Development Office
MARAD	Maritime Administration
NASA	National Aeronautics and Space Administration
NDGPS	Nationwide Differential Global Positioning System
NHTSA	National Highway Traffic Safety Administration
NIST	National Institute of Standards and Technology
NSF	National Science Foundation
NSTC	National Science and Technology Council
OPS	Office of Pipeline Safety
OST	Office of the Secretary of Transportation
PHMSA	Pipeline and Hazardous Materials Safety Administration
R&T	Research and Technology
RD&T	Research, Development, and Technology
REDAC	Research, Engineering, and Development Advisory Committee
RFID	Radiofrequency Identification
RITA	Research and Innovative Technology Administration
RSPA	Research and Special Programs Administration
TRB	Transportation Research Board
TSA	Transportation Security Administration
UTC	University Transportation Center

TABLE OF CONTENTS

Tables and Figures

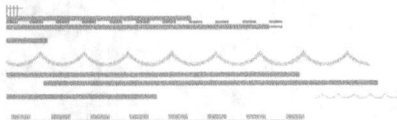

Introduction

> **RITA is the DOT administration primarily dedicated to RD&T coordination and management.**

The Norman Y. Mineta Research and Special Programs Improvement Act of 2004 was signed into law by President Bush on November 30, 2004. It embodies Secretary Mineta's vision of a Department-wide resource to guide the coordination and management of research, development, and technology (RD&T) activities. The Act dissolves the Research and Special Programs Administration (RSPA), creating in its stead two separate administrations: the Pipeline and Hazardous Materials Safety Administration (PHMSA) and the Research and Innovative Technology Administration (RITA). Through a realignment of other existing Department of Transportation (DOT) entities, RITA comprises offices with research and analytical capabilities that were previously fragmented. These include:

- The Office of Innovation, Research, and Education; the Volpe National Transportation Systems Center; and the Transportation Safety Institute, all previously in the former RSPA
- The Office of Intermodalism previously in the Office of the Secretary (OST)
- The Bureau of Transportation Statistics (BTS)

RITA Roles and Responsibilities

As envisioned by the Secretary, RITA is the DOT administration primarily dedicated to RD&T coordination and management. A committed crossmodal focus will ensure that RD&T investments are effective and tied to DOT's strategic goals. In particular, the Act assigns to the RITA Administrator responsibilities for:

- Coordination, facilitation, and review of DOT's portfolio of RD&T programs and activities
- Support and advancement of RD&T on innovative technologies, including intelligent transportation systems (ITS)
- Comprehensive transportation statistics research, collection, analysis, and reporting
- Education and training in transportation and transportation-related fields
- Activities of the Volpe National Transportation Systems Center

With the establishment of RITA, DOT is putting into place an integrated RD&T planning process aligned with the *DOT Strategic Plan*. The DOT operating administrations will continue to conduct RD&T based on their agency missions, interactions with stakeholders, and knowledge of transportation technologies and challenges.

Summary of Report

This document responds to Section 4(g) of the Act, which requires the RITA Administrator to submit a Report to Congress on DOT's current and projected RD&T priorities. This report was developed with broad stakeholder input obtained through a special session at the Transportation Research Board (TRB) annual meeting, a *Federal Register* notice, and a dedicated email address for receiving responses. It also considers the RD&T contributions of other organizations and addresses methods to avoid unnecessary duplication.

In preparing this report, RITA recognizes that the legislative effort to reauthorize the surface transportation program, which is now taking place in Congress, will give additional guidance and funding authorization to DOT's Federal Highway Administration (FHWA), Federal Motor Carrier Safety Administration (FMCSA), Federal Transit Administration (FTA), National Highway Traffic Safety Administration (NHTSA), and some portions of RITA. As such, the planning activities and processes described in this document are subject to change and refinement, and will reflect the directions provided by Congress when the legislation is enacted.

The remaining sections of this report are as follows:

Section 2—RITA's vision, mission, goals, and strategies

Section 3—RD&T priorities and purposes for 2003-2008 that guide DOT research and the FY 2006 programs that support them

Section 4—Crosscutting RD&T coordination and planning processes, including collaborative efforts with other agencies and stakeholders

Section 5—Conclusion

Appendix A—FY 2006 RD&T budget requests for DOT's operating administrations

Appendix B—Results of DOT reviews of operating administrations' FY 2005 RD&T programs

1 *Federal Register,* Vol. 70, No. 16
Wednesday, January 26, 2005.

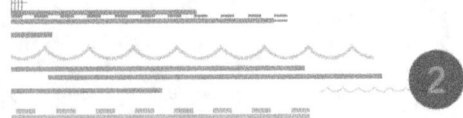

RITA Vision, Mission, Goals, & Strategies

Secretary Mineta's vision for RITA reflects its unique position in the Department: a crosscutting DOT administration dedicated solely to RD&T and the implementation of innovative technologies. RITA will provide counsel to the Secretary on innovation and research, and enable better coordination within the Department and with RD&T stakeholders.

RITA's mission reflects its legislative mandate and directly supports DOT's mission to "Develop and administer policies and programs that contribute to providing fast, safe, efficient, and convenient transportation at the lowest cost consistent with the national objectives of general welfare, economic growth and stability, the security of the United States and the efficient use and conservation of the resources of the United States."[2]

RITA's strategic goals respond to its mission and directly contribute to each of the Department's strategic objectives: safety, mobility, global connectivity, environmental stewardship, and security.

To realize its vision, mission, and goals, RITA proposes crosscutting strategies in the following areas:

- RD&T Strategic Planning, Review, and Coordination
- Innovation, Technology, and Enabling Research
- University Research and Education
- Transportation Statistics and Analysis

RD&T Strategic Planning, Review, and Coordination

Strategic Planning
RITA will lead the newly established RD&T Planning Council, and its Planning Team, to focus RD&T priorities (see Section 4). As a result of this planning process, RITA will develop both an annual RD&T plan and a multi-year RD&T strategic plan in consultation with stakeholders and the DOT operating administrations.

---

2 *DOT Strategic Plan 2003-2008*
p. 19.

RD&T Review

With support from RITA, the RD&T Planning Council and its Planning Team will annually review RD&T programs to ensure they implement the Administration's RD&T investment criteria. In addition, RITA will develop broad guidelines for program reviews conducted by advisory councils or other bodies, and summarize review results in the annual RD&T plan.

Crossmodal Coordination

RITA will facilitate coordination of RD&T in crossmodal areas such as hydrogen technology, remote sensing, and human factors. RITA will develop additional crossmodal working groups as needed, modeled on existing groups such as DOT's Human Factors Coordinating Committee (HFCC) and the Center for Climate Change and Environmental Forecasting. Finally, RITA will provide a clearinghouse for information on RD&T activities throughout the Department.

Intermodal RD&T

RITA will serve as DOT's principal advocate for, and advisor on, intermodal transportation RD&T. RITA will coordinate intermodal RD&T, both passenger and freight, including research needs identified by the RD&T Planning Council and the RD&T Planning Team.

Innovation, Technology, and Enabling Research

Innovation Gaps and Priorities

RITA will work with the RD&T Planning Council and the RD&T Planning Team to analyze priority transportation issues and identify innovation gaps. This effort will be closely integrated with the RD&T strategic planning process.

Technology Outreach and Partnerships

RITA will promote partnerships by facilitating outreach sessions on opportunities for public-private collaboration, facilitating RD&T partnerships with other agencies, and working with the DOT operating administrations to identify mutual RD&T opportunities.

Enabling Research

RITA will monitor research that supports long-term transportation advances—including work in the Department of Energy (DOE), the Department of Homeland Security (DHS), the National Aeronautics and Space Administration (NASA), the National Science Foundation (NSF), and other agencies—to identify opportunities for collaboration and apply results to crossmodal issues. RITA will also facilitate DOT participation in the National Science and Technology Council (NSTC), including such efforts as the National Nanotechnology Initiative and the Hydrogen Initiative.

International RD&T

RITA will disseminate information on DOT's international RD&T activities, facilitate information sharing with researchers in other countries, and monitor foreign research and technology. RITA will also work with the DOT operating administrations to identify new opportunities for transnational RD&T partnerships.

University Research and Education

University Research

RITA will continue RSPA's management of the University Transportation Centers (UTC) program. Authorized by TEA-21, the program uses Trust Fund money to support 26 university centers across the country. In addition to managing the UTC program, RITA will integrate information on DOT's various university activities.

Education and Workforce Development

RITA will work with partners in academia and industry to build the professional capacity of the transportation workforce. RITA's activities will complement the efforts of DOT's operating administrations by reaching out to the broader transportation and education communities. In addition, the Administration's proposal for reauthorization of surface transportation programs—the Safe, Accountable, Flexible, and Efficient Transportation Equity Act—includes a provision for a new Transportation Scholarship Opportunities Program that RITA will administer.

Transportation Statistics and Analysis

As part of RITA, BTS will continue its statistical functions as authorized by statute. The agency's current mandate covers all modes of transportation and calls for the collection and analysis of data on topics relevant to DOT's strategic goals. BTS's mission is threefold: collect, compile, analyze, and publish objective transportation statistics; improve the comparability and quality of these statistics; and promote improvements in transportation data acquisition, dissemination, and use.

BTS will continue to be a key resource for DOT's RD&T-performing administrations. The DOT operating administrations use BTS data and analysis to determine RD&T needs, priorities, and investment decisions. Stakeholders also rely on BTS data, which are transparent and follow quality guidelines for collection, compilation, and dissemination.

3

Research, Development, & Technology Priorities

The *DOT Strategic Plan 2003-2008* identifies five objectives that are the purpose for all RD&T in the Department:

- *Safety:* Enhance public health and safety by working toward the elimination of transportation-related deaths and injuries.
- *Mobility:* Advance accessible, efficient, intermodal transportation for the movement of people and goods.
- *Global Connectivity:* Facilitate a more efficient domestic and global transportation system that enables economic growth and development.
- *Environmental Stewardship:* Promote transportation solutions that enhance communities and protect the natural and built environment.
- *Security:* Balance homeland and national security transportation requirements with the mobility needs of the Nation for personal travel and commerce.

The *Strategic Plan* also defines a number of broad strategies to achieve these objectives, many of which are priorities for RD&T. These priorities, and the FY 2006 programs that support them, are identified in Tables 3-2 through 3-6. Several programs address more than one strategy or objective, such as the UTC program described on the next page. DOT's total FY 2006 budget request is shown in Table 3-1. (For more detailed budget and program information, see Appendix A and the 6th edition of DOT's *Research, Development, and Technology Plan.*)

The next *DOT Strategic Plan* is due to Congress in September 2006. As DOT revises the plan, RITA will work with the RD&T Planning Council, RD&T Planning Team, DOT operating administrations, and stakeholders to reassess RD&T priorities. These priorities will span the same period as the revised *Strategic Plan* (2006-2009).

Table 3-1. Summary of FY 2006 RD&T Budget Request ($000)

DOT Operating Administration	FY 2005 Enacted	FY 2006 Request
FAA	263,233	250,716
FHWA	601,857	572,206
FMCSA	10,516	13,068
FRA	59,831	51,166
FTA	61,166	54,419
NHTSA	93,844	99,006
OST	19,490	9,030
PHMSA	12,656	12,004
RITA	2,375	3,792
TOTAL DOT	1,124,968	1,065,407

DOT's University Transportation Centers Program

The UTC program invests in university-based centers of excellence to advance innovation, research, education, and technology transfer. The program is managed by RITA and funded by the FHWA and FTA. Each of the 26 current UTCs has a specific transportation theme that advances at least one of DOT's strategic objectives. The UTCs, their themes, and the primary DOT objectives they support are as follows:

City College of New York—Planning and Management of Regional Transportation Systems (Mobility)

George Mason University—Deployment of Intelligent Transportation Systems (Safety, Mobility)

Iowa State University—Sustainable Transportation Asset Management (Mobility, Environmental Stewardship)

Marshall University—Transportation and Economic Development in Mountain Regions (Mobility, Environmental Stewardship)

Massachusetts Institute of Technology—Strategic Management of Transportation Systems (Mobility)

Montana State University, Bozeman—Rural Travel and Transportation (Mobility)

North Dakota State University—Rural and Intermodal Transportation (Mobility)

Northwestern University—Infrastructure Technology (Mobility)

Pennsylvania State University—Advanced Technologies in Transportation Operations and Management (Safety, Mobility, Global Connectivity)

Rutgers University—Advanced Transportation Infrastructure: Maintenance and Operation of High-Volume Systems (Safety, Mobility)

San Jose State University—Policy Guidance of Transportation Management Systems (Mobility)

South Carolina State University—Professional Capacity Building in Transportation (Safety, Mobility)

Texas A&M University—Transportation Solutions to Enhance Prosperity and the Quality of Life (Mobility, Environmental Stewardship)

University of Alabama—Management and Safety of Transportation Systems (Safety)

University of Arkansas—Rural Transportation (Mobility)

University of California—Transportation Systems Analysis and Policy (Mobility, Environmental Stewardship)

University of Central Florida—Advanced Transportation Systems Simulation (Safety, Mobility, Security)

University of Idaho—Advanced Transportation Technology (Mobility, Environmental Stewardship)

University of Minnesota—Human-Centered Transportation Technology (Safety, Mobility)

University of Missouri, Rolla—Advanced Materials and Non-Destructive Testing Technologies (Mobility)

University of Rhode Island—Surface Intermodal Transportation Systems and Advanced Transportation Infrastructure with Special Reference to the Marine Environment (Mobility, Global Connectivity)

University of Southern California and California State University, Long Beach—Metropolitan Transportation (Mobility, Global Connectivity)

University of South Florida—Transit and Alternative Forms of Urban Transportation (Mobility)

University of Tennessee—Transportation Safety (Safety)

University of Washington—Transportation Operations and Planning (Mobility)

University of Wisconsin, Madison—Optimization of Transportation Investment and Operations (Mobility)

Safety RD&T: Human Factors Coordinating Committee

An example of the Department's safety RD&T is the work of the HFCC. Established by the Secretary in 1991, the HFCC identifies and coordinates crossmodal RD&T and ensures the appropriate application of the science of human factors to the design, development, implementation, and evaluation of transportation systems. A model for crossmodal planning—particularly for DOT's RD&T Planning Council and RD&T Planning Team—the HFCC provides a forum for collaboration among program managers from all operating administrations. It also coordinates with members from the Department of Defense (DOD), Transportation Security Administration (TSA), U.S. Coast Guard, National Institute for Occupational Safety and Health, National Transportation Safety Board, and other agencies. The HFCC chair is a two-year position that rotates among the member administrations.

In addition to providing a venue for information sharing, the HFCC looks for opportunities to leverage resources across modes to address common issues. A recent example is the HFCC's Operator Fatigue Management Program. Launched in 2000, this program has delivered three major products and is scheduled to deliver two more in 2005. These products are fatigue management tools that are crossmodal in their application and available to the end users. The suite of tools includes (1) a software application to aid managers and schedulers in evaluating and designing work schedules; (2) guidance for validating fatigue models for different uses; (3) a handbook of scientifically-based fatigue management practices and countermeasures; (4) a logic model framework for prioritizing fatigue research; and (5) a blueprint for deriving a business case for the implementation of fatigue management activities.

Safety

Safety is DOT's primary objective. Through RD&T efforts, the Department strives to improve the benefits of transportation while consistently reducing risks to the health and well-being of the public, the environment, and the economy. Working with stakeholders, DOT ensures that the technologies and techniques necessary to identify and resolve safety issues are developed, made available, and enforced. The *Strategic Plan* names the following RD&T priorities for safety:[3]

- Conducting, supporting, and publishing research in all modes on safety-enhancing technologies and on topics related to safety such as human performance, differing cultural norms, behavior, and unsafe trends
- Developing, promoting, and supporting public education and information activities that advance safe behavior, safe operations, and best safety practices
- Providing training and technical assistance to industry and state and local government agencies on safety issues and safety management practices
- Working with stakeholders to build safety into the transportation infrastructure and operational procedures through research, planning, design, engineering, incentives, and incorporation of safety-enhancing technologies
- Mitigating the consequences of safety incidents through more effective response, technology, and coordination with private transportation providers and state and local government
- Increasing implementation of infrastructure and operational improvements focused on enhancing drivers' abilities to remain on the roadway, reducing the adverse consequences of roadway departure, improving intersection safety, and protecting pedestrians in the roadway environment

3 ibid., pp. 22-23.

Table 3-2 shows the major FY 2006 RD&T activities that will support these priorities.

Table 3-2. FY 2006 RD&T Programs Supporting Safety

DOT-wide	Crossmodal Human Factors Research*
FAA	Advanced Technology Development and Prototyping
	Aircraft Safety Technology
	Airport Technology
	Aviation Weather Program
	Commercial Space Transportation
	Human Factors and Aerospace Medicine
FHWA	Highway Operations
	ITS Safety**
	Pavement Research
	Planning and Decision Making Research
	Safety Research and Technology
	Structures Research
	Training and Education
FMCSA	Produce Safer Drivers
	Improve Safety of Commercial Motor Vehicles
	Produce Safer Carriers
	Advance Safety through Information-Based Initiatives
	Improve Security through Safety Initiatives
	Enable and Motivate Internal Excellence
FRA	Grade Crossings
	Hazardous Materials Transportation
	Human Factors
	Nationwide Differential Global Positioning System (NDGPS)*
	R&D Facilities and Test Equipment
	Railroad System Issues
	Rolling Stock and Components
	Signal and Train Control
	Track and Structures
	Track and Train Interaction
	Train Occupant Protection
FTA	Safety and Security
NHTSA	Crash Avoidance
	Crashworthiness
	Data Programs
	Highway Safety Research
	Hydrogen Initiative
	Vehicle Research and Test Center
OST	Transportation Planning, Research, and Development*
PHMSA	Hazardous Materials Safety
	Pipeline Safety
RITA	Hydrogen R&D*

*Crossmodal.

**Indicates the historical location of the ITS program. Changes may result from Congressional direction established in the final passed surface transportation reauthorization. The ITS program involves several DOT operating administrations.

Mobility RD&T: Intelligent Transportation Systems

The ITS program is DOT's largest crossmodal initiative. This program supports mobility and other DOT objectives through the application of advanced technologies to surface transportation. Major elements include intelligent vehicles, commercial vehicle operations, transit systems, and ITS architecture. Policy guidance comes from the ITS Management Council, which is composed of senior leadership from across DOT. Recently, the Council reoriented the program to focus on a fewer number of higher-risk, high-payoff initiatives. These are:

- Integrated Vehicle Based Safety Systems

- Cooperative Intersection Collision Avoidance Systems

- Next Generation 9-1-1

- Mobility Services for All Americans

- Integrated Corridor Management Systems

- Nationwide Surface Transportation Weather Observing and Forecasting System—Clarus

- Emergency Transportation Operations

- Universal Electronic Freight Manifest

- Vehicle Infrastructure Integration

These initiatives and ongoing efforts—such as the Intelligent Vehicle Initiative and Commercial Vehicle Information Systems and Networks—depend on program funding and the passage of reauthorizing legislation. The ITS program will also conduct exploratory studies to assess promising, but as yet untested, ITS strategies.

Mobility

A nation's mobility is intertwined with its economic growth. The transportation system connects people with work, school, community services, markets, and other people. DOT's aim is to maintain and advance an affordable, reliable, and accessible transportation system. Toward this end, DOT RD&T addresses the following priorities:[4]

- Exploiting web-enabled and other secure information technologies to share information on best practices in all modes
- Examining ways to encourage cargo transport by water to improve the capacity of the intermodal transportation system[5]
- In consultation with public and private sector partners, conducting research and expediting the deployment of technologies that improve system efficiency and infrastructure durability
- Providing technical assistance and training to improve intermodal transportation planning and effective system management and operation

The RD&T efforts addressing DOT's mobility priorities are shown in Table 3-3.

4 ibid., pp. 32-33.

5 The Maritime Administration does not have funding considered as "RD&T." However, it does have RD&T-related efforts, which it undertakes in close cooperation with the maritime industry, academia, and other Federal agencies.

Table 3-3. FY 2006 RD&T Programs Supporting Mobility

FAA
Advanced Technology Development and Prototyping
Airport Technology
Environment and Energy
National Plan for Transformation of Air Transportation
Wake Turbulence

FHWA
Highway Operations
ITS Mobility*
ITS System Management Information*
Multimodal Research**
Pavement Research
Planning, Environment, and Realty
Policy Research
Structures Research
Training and Education

FRA
NDGPS
Signal and Train Control

FTA
Fleet Operations
Metropolitan and Rural Policy Development
National Transit Institute
Planning and Project Development
Specialized Customer Services
Transit Cooperative Research Program

MARAD*
Marine Transportation System
Cooperative Research Programs
Marine Energy and Emissions Technologies
Global Maritime and Transportation School Research and
  Special Projects

RITA
UTC Program**

*Indicates the historical location of the ITS program. Changes may result from Congressional direction established in the final passed surface transportation reauthorization. The ITS program involves several DOT operating administrations.
**Crossmodal.
***MARAD's RD&T-related efforts are not formally part of DOT's RD&T program.

Global Connectivity RD&T: National Freight Action Agenda

Globalization is putting pressure on the capacity of the Nation's ports, borders, and intermodal connections. DOT is responding to this challenge through a National Freight Action Agenda to increase capacity to move freight throughout the transportation system. The agenda identifies several high-priority freight initiatives, including the following RD&T projects:

Standardized Freight Communications: An ITS effort, this will promote a Dedicated Short-Range Communications service based on use of the 5.9 GHz radio frequency that has been newly designated for transportation. The service will support standardized communications for both roadside-to-vehicle and vehicle-to-vehicle freight operations.

Intelligent Railroad Systems: This FRA program will develop advanced sensing and communication technologies to increase safety and capacity, reduce system delays, and cut shipping costs. Major components include positive train control and installation of the NDGPS.

Universal Electronic Freight Manifest: Building on ITS operational tests, this effort will demonstrate use of a common freight manifest by all supply chain partners—manufacturers, shippers, freight forwarders, air carriers. With a standardized electronic format, shippers in all modes will have real-time access to critical information, including that needed for security screening.

Short Sea Shipping: Short Sea Shipping is the water transportation of freight and passengers that does not cross an ocean. Led by MARAD, this work will promote technologies leading to the accelerated deployment of Short Sea Shipping as a tool for reducing congestion and accommodating freight movement.

Radio-Frequency Identification (RFID): This program will promote expanded use of RFID tags, which can potentially provide perfect visibility along the supply chain. RITA will assess crossmodal RFID requirements, in cooperation with stakeholders and other agencies.

Global Connectivity

The increasingly global economy hinges on smooth supply chains and just-in-time manufacturing. Transportation is critical to both. An intermodal approach is central to DOT's role in promoting global connectivity. The following are the Department's RD&T priorities:[6]

- Encouraging and facilitating intermodal transportation planning worldwide
- Supporting and conducting research on issues concerning the intersection of passenger and freight transportation
- Accelerating the use of ITS and other technologies that reduce delays at key intermodal transfer points, in significant freight corridors, and at international border crossings

Table 3-4 presents the RD&T that supports these priorities.

6 ibid, pp. 44-45.

Table 3-4. FY 2006 RD&T Programs Supporting Global Connectivity

FHWA	ITS Freight* Planning and Decision Making Research Policy Research
FRA	Grade Crossings NDGPS Rolling Stock and Components Signal and Train Control
FTA	International Mass Transportation Program
MARAD	Short Sea Shipping Cooperative Program**
OST	Transportation Planning, Research, and Development***
RITA	Intermodalism***

*Indicates the historical location of the ITS program. Changes may result from Congressional direction established in the final passed surface transportation reauthorization. The ITS program involves several DOT operating administrations.
**This RD&T-related effort is not directly funded through DOT's RD&T program.
***Crossmodal.

Environmental RD&T: Crossmodal Initiatives

DOT Center for Climate Change and Environmental Forecasting: Led by the Office of the Assistant Secretary for Transportation Policy, this "virtual" center brings together all operating administrations to promote a better understanding of the links between transportation and greenhouse-gas emissions. Recently, the center completed a study of the greenhouse-gas-reduction potential of selected fuels, and initiated work on the impacts of climate change on the transportation system. The DOT operating administrations contribute staff and other resources and RITA provides administrative support to the center.

Hydrogen Fuels R&D: Part of the President's Hydrogen Fuel Initiative, this RITA-led program seeks to remove barriers to the widespread deployment of hydrogen-fueled vehicles. The program conducts research on (1) codes and standards for the safe handling and transport of large quantities of hydrogen fuel; and (2) the safety of on-board hydrogen vehicle power and storage systems.

Environmental Stewardship

Transportation exerts pressure on environmental resources worldwide. The *DOT Strategic Plan* calls for a balance between environmental challenges and the need for a safe and efficient transportation network. Among the RD&T priorities for achieving this vision are:[7]

- Supporting the President's Hydrogen Fuel Initiative through research on fuel distribution and delivery infrastructure, transportation of associated hazardous materials, and vehicle safety
- Supporting interdisciplinary research on connections among transportation, energy, and the environment
- Adopting transportation policies and promoting technologies that reduce or eliminate environmental degradation
- Collaborating with Federal agencies, academic institutions, and the private sector to support and conduct research on technologies that improve energy efficiency, foster the use of alternative fuels, and reduce vehicle emissions
- Working with transportation partners to mitigate the adverse environmental effects of existing transportation systems

The RD&T programs that address these priorities are listed in Table 3-5.

---

7 ibid, pp. 54-55.

Table 3-5. FY 2006 RD&T Programs Supporting Environmental Stewardship

DOT-wide	Crosscutting Environmental Issues*
	Center for Climate Change and Environmental Forecasting*
FAA	Environment and Energy
FHWA	Pavement Research
	Planning and Decision Making Research
	Planning, Environment, and Realty
FRA	Railroad System Issues
FTA	Equipment and Infrastructure
OST	Transportation Planning, Research, and Development*
PHMSA	Pipeline Safety
RITA	Hydrogen R&D*

*Crossmodal.

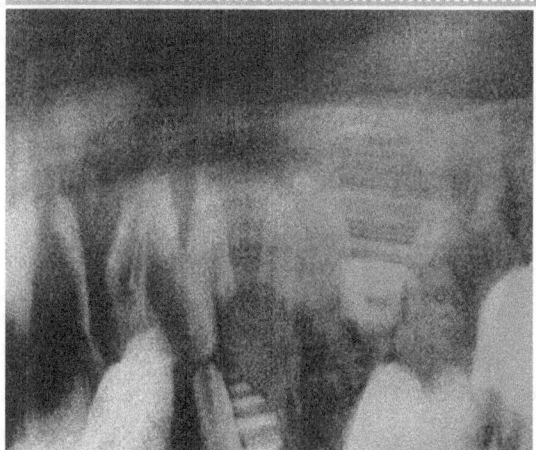

Security

The Nation's transportation system has vulnerabilities that need to be guarded against attack. The *DOT Strategic Plan* identifies strategies for working with the DHS and with state, local, and private sector partners to elevate security while improving safety and efficiency. RD&T priorities are:[8]

- Monitoring the transportation system 24/7 to provide real-time reports and help ensure rapid response and recovery from disruptions to transportation throughout the Nation
- Implementing cybersecurity programs to adequately protect DOT systems integrated with the national critical infrastructure
- Employing advancements in information and communications technology to improve the accuracy, speed, and simplicity of exchanging information on security, emergency response, and defense deployment with Federal, state, and local governments and with the private sector

Supporting RD&T is presented in Table 3-6.

8 ibid, pp. 62-63.

Table 3-6. FY 2006 RD&T Programs Supporting Security

FAA	Information Security—Orderly Quarantine*
FHWA	Highway Operations Structures Research
FMCSA	Improve Security through Safety Initiatives
FRA	NDGPS Railroad System Issues
FTA	Safety and Security

*Funded under the FAA's Facilities and Equipment program, this effort is not formally part of the RD&T program.

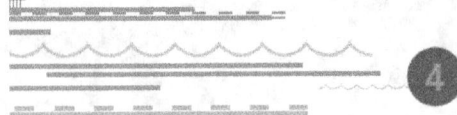

Research, Development, & Technology Strategic Planning

With the establishment of RITA, DOT is putting into place an integrated RD&T planning process aligned with the *DOT Strategic Plan*. This cyclical process tracks multi-year priorities with annual budgets and goals. Within this framework, DOT's operating administrations continue to conduct RD&T activities based on their agency missions, interactions with stakeholders, and knowledge of transportation technologies and challenges.

RITA works with the DOT operating administrations to define Departmental RD&T priorities and ensure program effectiveness. RITA also fosters collaboration in RD&T activities—within DOT; across the Government; and with partners in state and local agencies, not-for-profit institutions, academia, and industry.

To assist RITA with RD&T planning, the Department recently established two internal bodies:

- *RD&T Planning Council*: The RD&T Planning Council ensures crossmodal collaboration and coordination of RD&T within DOT and with external entities. Chaired by the RITA Administrator, the council comprises the heads of the operating administrations, the Under Secretary for Policy, and other senior leaders from the Office of the Secretary.

- *RD&T Planning Team*: The RD&T Planning Team assists the RD&T Planning Council and the RITA Administrator in ensuring crossmodal collaboration and coordination of RD&T. It is chaired by RITA's Associate Administrator for Research, Development, and Technology and includes the Associate Administrators for RD&T in the operating administrations (or their equivalent) and comparable officials from the Office of the Secretary.

Both the Planning Council and Planning Team collaborate with other DOT coordination bodies, such as the ITS Management Council, the HFCC, the Center for Climate Change and Environmental Forecasting, and the Hydrogen Working Group.

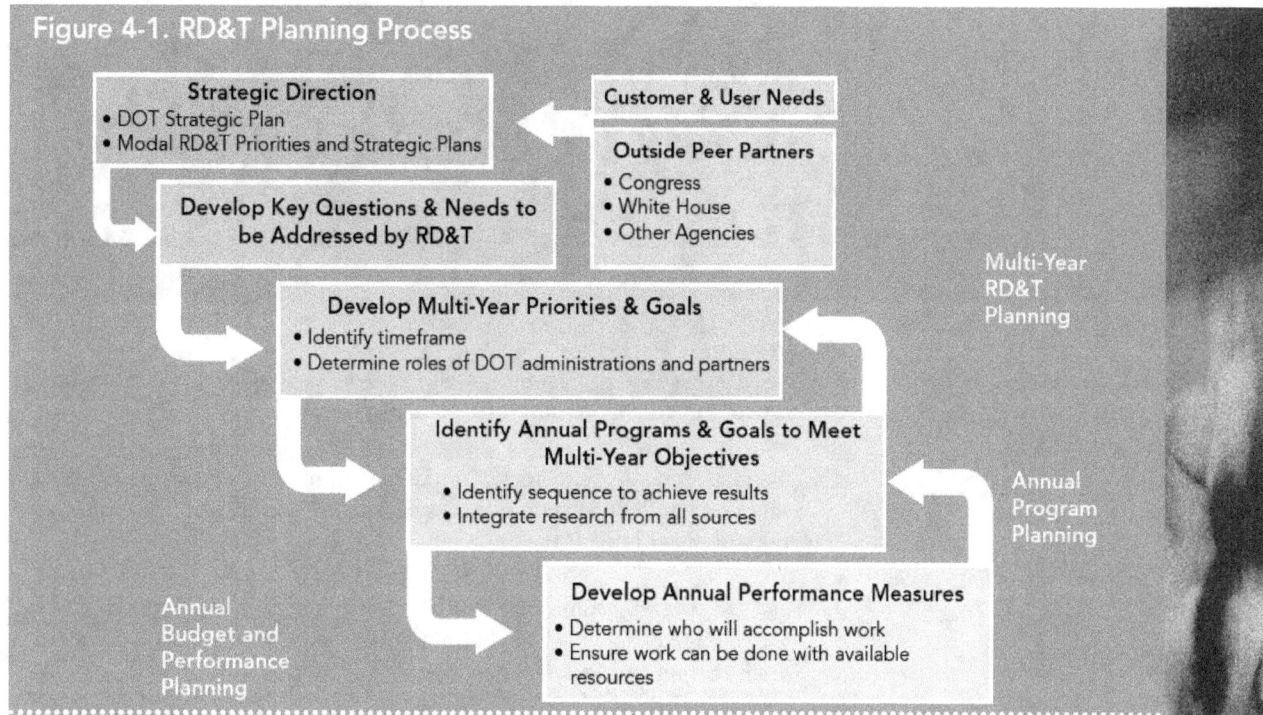

Figure 4-1. RD&T Planning Process

Strategic Direction
- DOT Strategic Plan
- Modal RD&T Priorities and Strategic Plans

Customer & User Needs

Outside Peer Partners
- Congress
- White House
- Other Agencies

Develop Key Questions & Needs to be Addressed by RD&T

Develop Multi-Year Priorities & Goals
- Identify timeframe
- Determine roles of DOT administrations and partners

Identify Annual Programs & Goals to Meet Multi-Year Objectives
- Identify sequence to achieve results
- Integrate research from all sources

Develop Annual Performance Measures
- Determine who will accomplish work
- Ensure work can be done with available resources

Multi-Year RD&T Planning

Annual Program Planning

Annual Budget and Performance Planning

Strategic Planning Process

As depicted in Figure 4-1, DOT's RD&T planning process has three elements: multi-year strategic planning, annual program planning, and budget and performance planning.

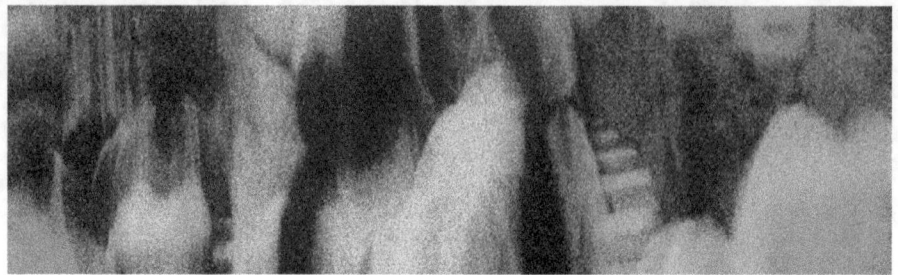

Multi-year Strategic Planning

RITA works with the RD&T Planning Council to define long-term, multi-year RD&T strategies for incorporation into DOT's *Strategic Plan*.

- Administration and Secretarial priorities are communicated through policy guidance from the RITA Administrator, the RD&T Planning Council, and the Under Secretary for Policy.

- The DOT operating administrations determine their individual priorities, based on mission requirements and customer needs, and how they can best address Administration and Secretarial priorities.

- The RD&T Planning Team develops recommendations for DOT-wide priorities for review by the Planning Council. In addition to Secretarial and operating administration priorities, these recommendations are based on the results of technology scans, stakeholder outreach, interactions with other agencies, and knowledge of emerging issues and problems. The approved RD&T priorities will be incorporated into the next *DOT Strategic Plan*.

- Working with DOT's operating administrations, RITA prepares a multi-year strategic RD&T plan that defines RD&T priorities and goals; supporting programs; and the roles of other agencies, state and local governments, and others.

RITA will complete a multi-year strategic RD&T plan by September 2006, when the next *DOT Strategic Plan* is submitted to Congress.

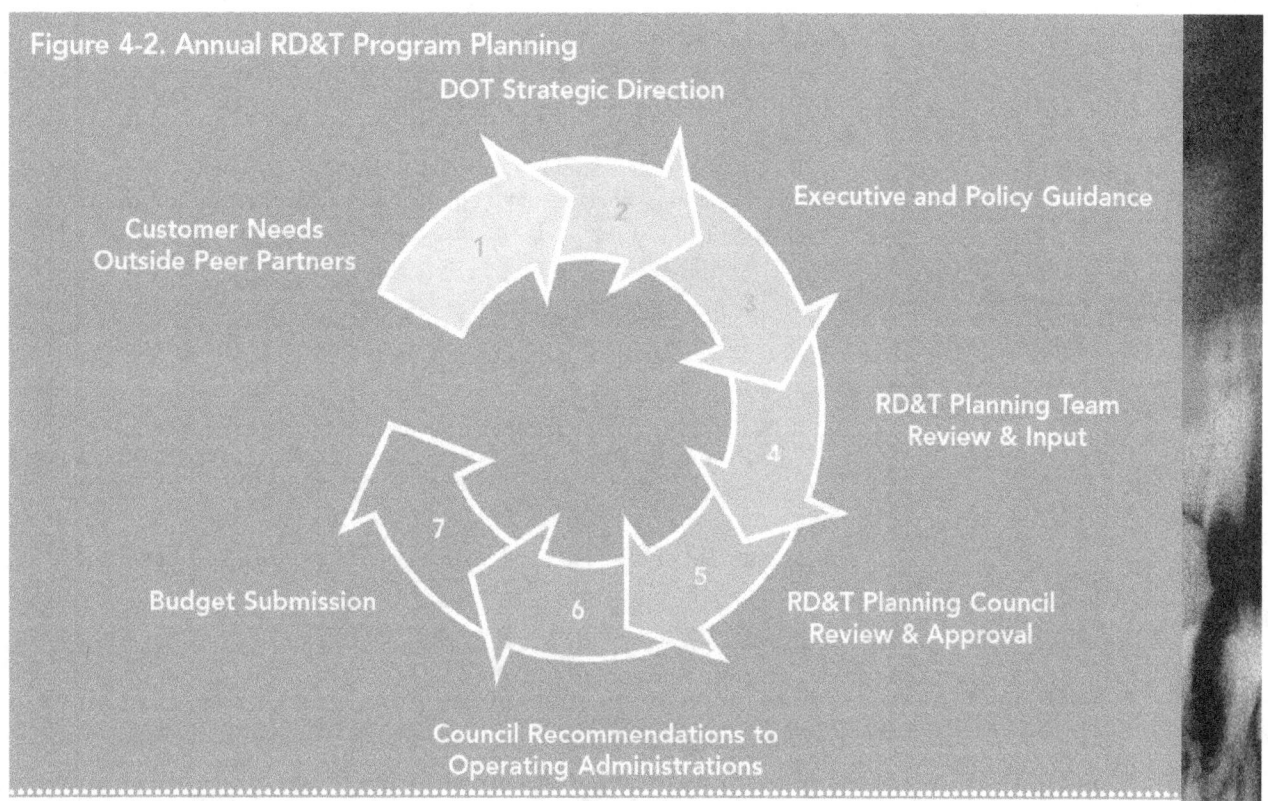

Figure 4-2. Annual RD&T Program Planning

DOT Strategic Direction

Customer Needs Outside Peer Partners

Executive and Policy Guidance

RD&T Planning Team Review & Input

Budget Submission

RD&T Planning Council Review & Approval

Council Recommendations to Operating Administrations

Annual Program Planning

Annual RD&T planning flows from DOT's multi-year planning and is linked to the budget process. Figure 4-2 shows the annual planning cycle.

- DOT's operating administrations determine their annual RD&T needs—based on mission requirements, customer needs, and interactions with outside peer partners—and how they will address Departmental priorities.

- Departmental priorities are communicated through executive and policy guidance from the Office of the Secretary based on the recommendations of the RITA Administrator and the RD&T Planning Council.

- Considering both DOT and operating administration priorities, the RD&T Planning Team develops recommendations for DOT-wide annual priorities and submits them to the RD&T Planning Council. Approved priorities are included in OST's budget guidance to the operating administrations for the upcoming fiscal year and in the annual RD&T plan submitted to Congress.

This annual process will be reflected in DOT's FY 2007 budget request and RD&T plan.

Budget and Performance Planning

RITA works with the RD&T Planning Council and RD&T Planning Team to support RD&T budgeting and performance assessment:

- RITA supports the Planning Council and Planning Team in assessing operating administrations' implementation of the Administration's RD&T investment criteria. This process builds on program reviews held for FY 2005. (See Appendix B.)

- RITA assists the RD&T Planning Team in the review of RD&T budgets to ensure consistency with Departmental priorities.

- RITA works with the Office of Management and Budget to ensure that RD&T performance mandates are met and that performance plans include measures and targets for RD&T.

Implementation of this process has already begun for the FY 2007 RD&T budget cycle.

Coordination with Stakeholders

Regular communication with stakeholders is an underlying element of DOT's entire RD&T planning process. At both the Departmental level and in the DOT operating administrations, such efforts ensure the effectiveness of RD&T and avoid unnecessary duplication.

DOT-wide External Coordination

Most recently, DOT solicited input from a range of stakeholders in preparing this Report to Congress. Stakeholder views were obtained through three means: a "Listening Session" hosted by the RSPA Deputy Administrator on January 10 in conjunction with the TRB annual meeting; a notice in the *Federal Register* on January 26; and a dedicated email address. The accompanying box summarizes these outreach efforts.

Stakeholder Input to the RITA Report

As required by the Mineta Act, this Report to Congress was developed with input from a wide range of stakeholders—including Federal, state, and local agencies; not-for-profit institutions; and the private sector.

On January 10, DOT held a "Listening Session" at the TRB annual meeting to solicit comments on the DOT reorganization and the roles of RITA. At the session, Chief of Staff John Flaherty and Deputy RSPA Director Samuel Bonasso presented their visions for RITA and asked for feedback. TRB Executive Director Robert Skinner opened the discussion by suggesting seven criteria by which to judge the new agency's success or failure: stakeholder involvement, balance between long- and short-term research, internal coordination and leadership, coordination with stakeholders and other agencies, R&D quality, scale of R&D efforts, and private sector participation.

In addition to the TRB session, the Department published a notice in the January 26th *Federal Register* and established an email address for responses. The notice asked for stakeholder input on the following questions:

Identification of Priorities
- How does DOT establish transportation research priorities in an environment of limited resources?
- How does DOT balance research on long-term, high-risk, and high-impact advances versus research with immediate transportation safety and mobility returns?

Research Duplication
- How does DOT identify and avoid unnecessary duplication in transportation-related technology research?
- How does DOT share information and learn about opportunities to benefit from others' research?

The Role of Stakeholders
- What ongoing communications methods or processes might be established with stakeholders outside of DOT to receive their advice and recommendations?
- What information resources can RITA utilize or create to leverage private sector advances into DOT missions and goals?

RITA has incorporated responses to these questions in the strategies and processes presented in this report. RITA will continue to work closely with stakeholders as it implements and refines these RD&T strategies and crossmodal planning efforts.

External Coordination in the DOT Operating Administrations

Within DOT's operating administrations, stakeholder input and review are essential for establishing RD&T priorities and programs. Examples of these activities include:

- *FAA*: One way in which the FAA ensures RD&T effectiveness is its Research, Engineering, and Development Advisory Committee (REDAC). Established by Congress in 1989, this committee reports to the FAA Administrator on RD&T issues and provides a link between agency research and similar efforts in industry, academia, and government. The committee meets twice a year with FAA senior managers and annually reviews the FAA's RD&T budget. Members represent corporations, universities, associations, consumers, and other agencies. Another body, the Commercial Space Transportation Advisory Committee, advises on RD&T in commercial space transportation safety.

- *FHWA*: In the FHWA, the TRB Research and Technology Coordinating Committee reviews RD&T, advises on research activities, and provides policy-level recommendations on program direction. The committee consists of 18 members from the states, academia, and private sector. The FHWA also has broad interaction with stakeholder groups, such as the Association of American State Highway and Transportation Officials, and engages customers throughout the RD&T planning process. For stakeholder input to the ITS program, the FHWA had previously relied on ITS America as a Utilized Federal Advisory Committee. The Department has determined that this program has matured to the point where a formal DOT Advisory Committee is needed, and is in the process of establishing such a body.

- *FMCSA*: The FMCSA gets input on its Research and Technology (R&T) Program from various stakeholders, including the National Transportation Safety Board, safety advocacy groups, the national enforcement community, the motor carrier industry, commercial driver groups, truck manufacturers, the driver training community, sleep researchers, insurance representatives, truck manufacturers, and the motor coach industry. The agency holds annual stakeholder forums to solicit recommendations for R&T projects and improved program planning. This input is reflected in a recently completed 5-year strategic plan and in annual budget submissions.

- *FRA*: FRA research is guided by both internal and external stakeholders, including the FRA Office of Safety, the Association of American Railroads, the American Public Transportation Association, the Highway–Railroad Grade Crossing Research Needs Conference, and state transportation officials. External review is provided by the TRB Committee for Review of the FRA Research, Development, and Demonstration Programs. This committee—which represents states, railroads, labor unions, universities, and financial institutions—annually assesses all FRA RD&T programs.

- *FTA*: Formed in October 2003 under the TRB, the FTA's Transit Research Analysis Committee assesses research needs and advises the agency on (1) the Federal role in transit research; (2) high-priority research opportunities; and (3) processes for ensuring that the FTA receives input and cooperation from stakeholders. Members represent transit authorities, community service agencies, state DOTs, research institutes, consulting firms, and equipment manufacturers.

- *MARAD*: Although MARAD receives no direct RD&T funding, the agency works closely with stakeholders to stimulate innovation through collaborative efforts such as the Marine Transportation System initiative, the Short Sea Shipping Cooperative Program, the Ship Operations Cooperative Program, the Marine Energy and Emissions Technologies Program, and several other cooperative research programs. This approach brings together the maritime industry, academia, and agencies to identify, coordinate, facilitate, and accomplish maritime RD&T. Recommendations for future research also come from the Marine Transportation System National Advisory Council, a Federal Advisory Council to MARAD.

- *NHTSA*: NHTSA assures the quality and effectiveness of its research through several means, including regular public meetings with stakeholders. Such meetings provide a forum in which researchers can present their work, respond to comments, and obtain broad input on the agency's RD&T program.

- *PHMSA*: PHMSA's pipeline safety program relies on stakeholder involvement, including R&D Forums and meetings of a Blue Ribbon Panel, to make sure that RD&T is aligned with the pipeline safety mission, makes use of the best available knowledge and expertise, and considers stakeholder perspectives. Stakeholders represented include Federal and state agencies, industry, pipeline trade associations, and standards organizations. The PHMSA Office of Hazardous Materials Safety conducts its RD&T activities in consultation with other agencies, state and local governments, international organizations, the regulated industry, and the interested public.

- *RITA*: RITA will work with stakeholders to ensure the effectiveness of its RD&T planning efforts and to identify RD&T priorities. In addition, RITA will rely on the Advisory Council for Transportation Statistics for advice on the quality and objectivity of BTS data and analyses.

Interagency Coordination

As the agency with the most direct responsibility for transportation, DOT leads transportation RD&T in the Government. To further this role, RITA works closely with other agencies to avoid research duplication and leverage Federal investments.

Departmental-level RD&T Coordination

At the Federal level, DOT coordinates RD&T with other agencies through the White House Office of Science and Technology Policy and the NSTC. Chaired by the President, the NSTC is a cabinet-level council that coordinates science and technology policies across the Government. Within DOT, RITA's role is to facilitate participation in NSTC initiatives—including the National Nanotechnology Initiative, Hydrogen Initiative, Manufacturing R&D Initiative, and National Imagery Initiative—to leverage agencies' research investments and to communicate DOT RD&T needs.

Operating Administration Coordination and Partnerships

DOT's operating administrations coordinate with other agencies in specific areas of mutual interest. Among the agencies with which the administrations collaborate are the following:

- *Department of Commerce*: Within the Department of Commerce (DOC), a number of agencies conduct research relevant to transportation. Current DOT efforts with DOC include: (1) FHWA work with the National Institute of Standards and Technology (NIST) on high-performance concrete; (2) FHWA-National Weather Service research on road weather observations; (3) an FRA-NIST effort on the fire safety of passenger rail car materials; and (4) the Joint Planning and Development Office (JPDO), through which the FAA, DOC, NASA, DOD, and DHS are defining the future air transportation system.

- *Department of Defense*: The DOD accounts for a large proportion of all Federal RD&T. Examples of collaborative work with DOT include: (1) FHWA-U.S. Army Corps of Engineers studies on concrete curing and pavement performance; (2) FHWA work with the Navy on high-performance steel for bridges; (3) the FAA-NASA-DOD Aviation Safety Program; (4) FRA work on a Rail Car Inspection Guide for the military through DOD's Technical Support Working Group; and (5) the JPDO.

- *Department of Energy*: The DOE conducts research in alternative fuels, propulsion systems, and related technologies. Current DOT-DOE efforts include: (1) joint implementation of the President's Hydrogen Fuel Initiative; (2) FAA work with Sandia National Laboratories' Airworthiness Assurance "Center of Excellence"; and (3) joint demonstrations and tests of technologies for detecting chemical, biological, and explosive agents.

- *Department of Homeland Security*: DOT collaboration with the DHS includes: (1) Operation Safe Commerce, a public–private partnership providing a test-bed for technologies that increase container security; (2) FRA-DHS research on the real-time tracking of hazardous-materials tank cars and the development of a rail addendum to the overall DOT-DHS Memorandum of Understanding; (3) FMCSA-TSA efforts on two projects: Untethered Trailer Tracking and Commercial Vehicle Information Systems and Networks; (4) FHWA support for development of an advanced Driver Training Range at the Federal Law Enforcement Training Center; and (5) FAA-DHS collaboration through the JPDO.

- *National Aeronautics and Space Administration*: NASA and the FAA are full research partners. Examples include: (1) coordination at the senior management level through the FAA-NASA Executive Committee; (2) working-level coordination through the Interagency Air Traffic Management Integrated Product Team and the FAA-NASA Aviation Safety Program; (3) joint meetings of NASA's and FAA's research advisory committees; (4) FAA-NASA research on aircraft noise and emissions reduction; and (5) joint development of technologies for the future air transportation system through the JPDO. In addition to NASA's work with the FAA, the agency cooperates with RITA on the transportation remote sensing program described in the box above.

- *National Science Foundation*: An independent agency, the NSF seeks to strengthen U.S. science and engineering through education and research. The NSF also engages in cooperative research, such as (1) a DOT-NSF Partnership for Research in Information and Communications Systems for Surface Transportation; and (2) a project with the FHWA and state DOTs on the long-term durability of materials and structures.

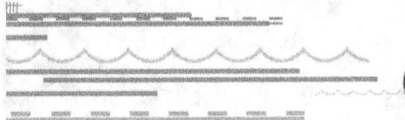

5 Conclusion

As envisioned by Secretary Mineta, RITA will be a Departmental resource for guiding the coordination and management of DOT's diverse RD&T portfolio. RITA will work with the DOT operating administrations to ensure that RD&T initiatives reflect sound investment decisions that clearly support Departmental objectives. In turn, such RD&T investments will lead to a better, more efficient national transportation system for the future.

RITA will implement a number of crosscutting strategies to further its mission to facilitate solutions to America's transportation challenges. These strategies will support a DOT-wide process that will ensure RD&T effectiveness, eliminate unnecessary duplication, and accelerate transportation innovations. RITA looks forward to implementing this process as it works with the DOT operating administrations, Congress, and stakeholders to build a transportation system that will support the Nation's future economic growth and prosperity.

Operating Administration and Program	FY 2005 Enacted	FY 2006 Budget
FHWA		
Surface Transportation Research	**101,779**	**199,000**
a. Safety	9,697	28,756
Safety (T)	1,711	5,074
b. Pavements	15,872	10,051
c. Structures	12,221	25,276
Structures (T)	1,667	3,447
d. Policy	8,928	12,940
e. Environmental, Planning, and Realty	11,366	25,711
Environmental, Planning, and Realty (T)	5,349	12,099
f. Highway Operations	7,738	19,104
Highway Operations (T)	5,158	12,736
g. R&T Technical Support	7,936	10,130
h. Long-Term Pavement Performance	9,920	15,488
i. Advanced Research	744	0
j. R&T Strategic Plan/Performance Measures	744	0
k. Asset Management	2,728	5,438
l. Field Services & Delivery	0	5,970
m. Resource Centers	0	4,000

n.	Corporate Centers	0	2,780
Technology Deployment Program		**49,600**	**0**
a.	Technology Deployment (T)	49,600	0
Training and Education		**19,840**	**26,000**
a.	National Highway Institute (T)	7,936	9,805
b.	Local Technical Assistance Program (T)	9,920	12,697
c.	Eisenhower Transportation Fellowship Program	1,984	3,498
Intelligent Transportation Systems		**230,144**	**121,000**
a.	Research	51,584	0
b.	Operational Test	9,920	0
c.	Architecture and Standards (T)	17,856	15,000
d.	ITS Program Support	11,408	9,000
e.	Integration/Deployment Support (T)	11,408	10,000
f.	ITS Deployment (T)	121,024	0
g.	Security	0	5,000
h.	Safety	0	38,000
i.	Mobility	0	24,000
j.	System Management Information (T)	0	14,000
k.	Evaluation (T)	6,944	6,000
University Transportation Research		**26,288**	**26,500**
a.	University Transportation Research (T)	26,288	26,500

A-1. FY 2006 BUDGET REQUEST FOR RESEARCH, DEVELOPMENT, AND TECHNOLOGY ($000)

Operating Administration and Program	FY 2005 Enacted	FY 2006 Budget
Multimodal Research	0	25,000
Other	157,545	157,545
a. State Planning & Research	157,545	157,545
Administrative Expenses	16,661	17,161
Subtotal, R&D	336,996	444,848
Subtotal, Technology Investment (T)	264,861	127,358
Subtotal, Facilities (F)	0	0
Total FHWA	601,857	572,206
FMCSA		
Motor Carrier Safety	10,516	13,068
Produce Safer Drivers	2,750	4,845
a. Produce Safer Drivers	2,750	4,585
b. Produce Safer Drivers (T)	0	260
Improve Safety of Commercial Motor Vehicles	2,777	2,960
a. Improve Safety of Commercial Motor Vehicles	1,777	460
b. Improve Safety of Commercial Motor Vehicles (T)	1,000	2,500
Produce Safer Carriers	120	880
a. Produce Safer Carriers	120	880
b. Produce Safer Carriers (T)	0	0
Advance Safety Through Information-Based Initiatives	1,035	1,498
a. Advance Safety Through Information-Based Initiatives	460	823

b.	Advance Safety Through Information-Based Initiatives (T)	575	675
Improve Security Through Safety Initiatives		500	300
a.	Improve Security Through Safety Initiatives	0	300
b.	Improve Security Through Safety Initiatives (T)	500	0
Enable and Motivate Internal Excellence		1,250	470
a.	Enable and Motivate Internal Excellence	1,150	470
b.	Enable and Motivate Internal Excellence (T)	100	0
Administrative Expenses		2,084	2,115
Subtotal, R&D		8,341	9,633
Subtotal, Technology Investment (T)		2,175	3,435
Subtotal, Facilities (F)		0	0
Total FMCSA		10,516	13,068
NHTSA			
Research and Analysis		69,648	72,936
Crashworthiness		25,360	23,693
a.	Safety Systems	9,186	9,318
b.	Biomechanics	16,174	14,375
Crash Avoidance		9,823	9,803
a.	Driver/Vehicle Performance	3,499	7,050
b.	Driver Behavior Simulation Research	0	0
c.	National Advanced Driver Simulator	3,605	0

A-1. FY 2006 BUDGET REQUEST FOR RESEARCH, DEVELOPMENT, AND TECHNOLOGY ($000)

Operating Administration and Program	FY 2005 Enacted	FY 2006 Budget
d. Heavy Vehicles	2,106	2,132
e. Pneumatic Tire Research	613	621
Data Programs (T)	32,713	36,570
a. Fatal Accident Reporting System (T)	6,566	7,063
b. National Accident Sampling System (NASS) (T)	12,080	12,230
c. Data Analysis Program (T)	1,975	2,023
d. State Data Program (T)	2,511	2,542
e. Occupant Protection Survey (T)	0	0
f. Special Crash Investigations (T)	1,679	1,712
g. National Motor Vehicle Crash Causation Survey (T)	6,914	10,000
h. Early Fatality Notification System (T)	988	1,000
Crash Avoidance Initiative	494	500
Vehicle Research and Test Center	1,008	1,020
Hydrogen Initiative	0	1,350
NAS Tire Study	250	0
Highway Safety Research	4,571	3,389
Administrative Expenses	19,625	22,681
Subtotal, R&D	61,131	62,436
Subtotal, Technology Investment (T)	32,713	36,570
Subtotal, Facilities (F)	0	0
Total NHTSA	93,844	99,006

FRA		
Railroad Research and Development	**35,737**	**46,325**
a. Railroad System Issues	3,001	2,952
b. Human Factors	3,422	3,366
c. Rolling Stock and Components	2,510	2,469
d. Track and Structures	3,670	3,366
Marshall U./U. of Nebraska	1,984	0
e. Track and Train Interaction	3,175	3,124
f. Train Control	893	880
g. Grade Crossings	1,885	1,854
h. Hazardous Materials Transportation	967	952
i. Train Occupant Protection	6,150	6,050
j. R&D Facilities and Test Equipment (F)	1,334	1,312
k. NDGPS (T)	6,746	20,000
Next Generation High-Speed Rail	**19,493**	**0**
a. HS Train Control Systems (T)	7,440	0
b. Non-Electric Locomotives (T)	1,687	0
c. Grade Crossing & Innovative Technologies (T)	4,315	0
d. Track/Structures Technology (T)	992	0
e. Corridor Planning (T)	3,075	0

A-1. FY 2006 BUDGET REQUEST FOR RESEARCH, DEVELOPMENT, AND TECHNOLOGY ($000)

Operating Administration and Program	FY 2005 Enacted	FY 2006 Budget
f. MAGLEV (T)	1,984	0
Safety and Operations	4,601	4,841
a. Salaries and Expenses (R&D)	3,537	3,742
b. Salaries and Expenses (T)	1,064	1,099
Subtotal, R&D	31,194	28,755
Subtotal, Technology Investment (T)	27,303	21,099
Subtotal, Facilities (F)	1,334	1,312
Total FRA	59,831	51,166
FTA		
Transit Planning and Research	54,660	47,892
National Program	37,300	34,515
Safety and Security	9,002	12,248
a. Safety and Security	0	0
b. Safety and Security (T)	9,002	12,248
Equipment and Infrastructure	6,920	2,785
a. New Bus and Rail Vehicles and Infrastructure	4,652	1,500
b. New Bus and Rail Vehicles and Infrastructure (T)	2,268	1,285
Fleet Operations	3,132	2,450
a. Bus Rapid Transit	1,932	0
b. Bus Rapid Transit (T)	1,200	2,450
Specialized Customer Services (T)	8,099	7,250

Information Management Technology	3,700	1,387
a. Information Management & Technology	0	0
b. Information Management & Technology (T)	3,700	1,387
Metropolitan/Rural Policy Development	885	1,295
a. Metropolitan/Rural Policy Development	300	300
b. Metropolitan/Rural Policy Development (T)	585	995
Planning and Project Development	3,690	3,600
a. Planning and Project Development	0	0
b. Planning and Project Development (T)	3,690	3,600
Human Resources (T)	885	1,600
Performance and Review	587	1,200
a. Performance and Review	187	0
b. Performance and Review (T)	400	1,200
International Mass Transportation Program (T)	400	700
Transit Cooperative Research Program	8,184	9,009
a. Transit Cooperative Research Program	0	0
b. Transit Cooperative Research Program (T)	8,184	9,009
National Transit Institute (T)	3,968	4,368
Rural Transit Assistance Program (T)	5,208	0
University Transportation Centers	6,000	6,000
a. University Transportation Centers	0	0

Operating Administration and Program	FY 2005 Enacted	FY 2006 Budget
b. University Transportation Centers (T)	6,000	6,000
Administrative Expenses	506	527
Subtotal, R&D	7,577	2,327
Subtotal, Technology Investment (T)	53,589	52,092
Subtotal, Facilities (F)	0	0
Total FTA	61,166	54,419
FAA		
Research, Engineering and Development	129,880	130,000
System Development and Infrastructure	3,878	4,664
a. System Planning and Resource Management	516	1,271
b. WJHTC Laboratory Facility	3,362	3,393
Weather	20,671	20,582
a. Weather Program	20,671	20,582
Aircraft Safety Technology	53,045	43,626
a. Fire Research and Safety	6,525	6,244
b. Advanced Materials/Structural Safety	6,643	2,613
c. Propulsion and Fuel Systems	7,115	4,049
d. Flight Safety/Atmospheric Hazards Research	4,086	3,441
e. Aging Aircraft	18,998	19,007
f. Aircraft Catastrophic Failure Prevention Research	1,107	3,340
g. Aviation Safety Risk Analysis	8,571	4,932

Human Factors (HF) and Aviation Medicine	31,170	24,724
a. Flight Deck/Maintenance/System Integration HF	11,700	8,181
b. Air Traffic Control/Airway Facilities HF	9,391	9,654
c. Aeromedical Research	10,079	6,889
Improve Efficiency	9,321	20,396
a. National Plan for Transformation of Air Transportation	5,059	18,100
b. Wake Turbulence	4,262	2,296
Environment and Energy	11,795	16,008
Facilities and Equipment	119,863	89,510
Advanced Technology Dev. & Prototyping	102,701	71,410
Plant (F)	17,162	18,100
Airport Technology (T)	0	17,500
Operations	13,380	13,581
Commercial Space Transportation	110	125
Subtotal, R&D	246,071	215,116
Subtotal, Technology Investment (T)	0	17,500
Subtotal, Facilities (F)	17,162	18,100
Total FAA	263,233	250,716
PHMSA		
Research and Special Programs	3,065	0
a. Hazardous Materials	1,831	0

Operating Administration and Program	FY 2005 Enacted	FY 2006 Budget
b. Research and Technology	374	0
c. Administrative Expenses	860	0
Hazardous Materials Safety	0	1,847
Administrative Expenses	0	464
Pipeline Safety	9,591	9,693
a. Pipeline Safety	8,986	9,067
b. Administrative Expenses	605	626
Total PHMSA	**12,656**	**12,004**
RITA		
Hazardous Materials R&D	54	80
Hydrogen R&D	335	1,000
R&D Planning and Management	362	541
Administrative Expenses	1,624	2,171
Total RITA	**2,375**	**3,792**
OST		
Transportation Planning, Research & Development	19,490	9,030
Total OST	**19,490**	**9,030**

TOTAL DOT		
R&D	725,831	787,941
Technology Investment (T)	380,641	258,054
Facilities (F)	18,496	19,412
GRAND TOTAL	1,124,968	1,065,407

Table B-1. Review of FAA RD&T Program

Investment Criterion	Program Evidence
Relevance	• Goals, priorities, and benefits are laid out in the *National Aviation Research Plan* and the *R&D Strategy*; these support both the FAA and DOT strategic plans. • Relevance is assessed both prospectively and retrospectively through the REDAC and other external review mechanisms. • Within the FAA, researchers work closely with agency customers to ensure the continuing relevance of research products.
Quality	• The FAA uses both an external and an internal peer-review process to ensure quality. • Managers prepare and vet program plans through a process that ensures good science and proper use of public funds. • Program quality is assessed retrospectively through the REDAC and other regular and ad hoc reviews.
Performance	• The program has long-term performance measures tied to specific research projects that support accomplishment of national and agency goals. • The program has annual performance measures that can demonstrate progress toward long-term goals. • Performance is documented in an annual performance plan and in quarterly and annual performance plan goal reports.

Table B-2. Review of FHWA RD&T Program

Investment Criterion	Program Evidence
Relevance	• Research program is mission-oriented and supports FHWA and DOT goals.
	• Stakeholders are engaged throughout the R&T process, including agenda setting and planning.
	• Stakeholders are involved in agenda setting and planning through the TRB Research and Technology Coordinating Committee, the National Partnership Initiative, and other advisory groups.
	• Stakeholders are engaged in the development of multi-year program plans, which are revisited annually.
	• External experts and advisory groups ensure program relevance throughout the research process itself.
	• Stakeholders are engaged in technology transfer and innovation delivery activities.
	• The program employs a number of mechanisms for customer feedback, including surveys and focus groups.
Quality	• Investment decisions are based on competition and merit review whenever possible.
	• External experts are consulted frequently during the conduct of research; merit reviews of results are encouraged.
	• An assessment process for the FHWA's 24 laboratories provides independent expert evaluation of research efforts.
Performance	• Stakeholders are involved in reviewing performance retrospectively.
	• The FHWA has conducted cost-benefit studies for elements of the program.
	• Program results are linked to the FHWA and DOT performance plans.
	• Performance is documented in an annual performance report.

Table B-3. Review of FMCSA R&T Program

Investment Criterion	Program Evidence
Relevance	• Research supports both FMCSA and DOT safety goals. • Customers and stakeholders are involved in developing and updating the FMCSA *5-Year R&T Strategic Plan*. • Program managers work closely with committees and research boards, including the TRB and the Association of American State Highway and Transportation Officials. • An intermodal management council sets priorities for ITS activities. • Several research projects are carried out in partnership with industry.
Quality	• Annual stakeholder forums afford customer review of research quality. • Expert panels review selected research projects. • Research is peer-reviewed internally and assessed at the program level. • All procurements specify that support for FMCSA goals is a requirement.
Performance	• Performance is linked to FMCSA and DOT goals and documented annually in the Department's performance plan. • Quantitative indicators include the number of studies developed, papers presented, and technologies under evaluation. • Cost-benefit analyses assess the performance of the ITS elements of the program.

Table B-4. Review of FRA RD&T Program

Investment Criterion	Program Evidence
Relevance	• All program elements contribute to Departmental and FRA goals.
	• Developed with other DOT agencies and key stakeholders, a five-year strategic plan outlines a vision for the future and the technologies needed to realize it.
	• The TRB Committee for Review of the FRA Research, Development, and Demonstration Programs provides annual prospective and retrospective review.
	• Other inputs to the RD&T planning process include coordination with the FRA's Office of Safety, the American Public Transportation Association Research Needs Conference, the Highway–Railroad Grade Crossing Research Needs Conference, and the Association of American Railroads Railway Technology Working Committee and Tank Car Committee.
Quality	• The FRA awards research contracts and grants on a competitive basis to the greatest extent possible.
	• The TRB conducts periodic peer reviews of FRA programs that address (1) the management structure and approach; (2) the direction and allocation of funds; and (3) the appropriate balance of Federal, state, and private sector inputs and costs.
Performance	• Inputs are tracked via an annual procurement plan; monthly obligations reports; and monthly progress reports that track actual vs. planned technical accomplishments, costs, and schedules.
	• All FRA RD&T contributes to the goals in the FRA's and Department's annual performance plans; the FRA is developing annual and long-term measures and targets to accurately assess the progress of its RD&T in meeting these goals.
	• The *DOT Performance and Accountability Report* provides a public accounting of FRA performance against the goals in the previous year's performance plan.

Table B-5. Review of FTA RD&T Program

Investment Criterion	Program Evidence
Relevance	• Research program is mission-oriented and supports FTA and DOT strategic goals.
	• Stakeholders are engaged throughout the process, including agenda setting and planning.
	• Program managers work closely with committees and research boards, including the TRB and organizations such as the American Public Transportation Association.
	• Stakeholders are involved in agenda setting and planning through the TRB's Transit Research Analysis Committee.
	• Stakeholders are engaged in the development of a Strategic Transit Research Plan.
	• External experts and advisory groups ensure program relevance throughout the research process itself.
	• Stakeholders are engaged in technology transfer and innovation delivery activities.
	• Prospective projects are evaluated on a scorecard system that incorporates the relevance criterion of the RD&T investment criteria.
Quality	• Investment decisions are based on competition and merit review whenever possible.
	• External experts are frequently consulted during the conduct of research; merit reviews of results are encouraged.
Performance	• Stakeholders are involved in reviewing performance retrospectively.
	• Program results are linked to the FTA and DOT performance plans.
	• All research projects are required to obtain approval of their performance measurement plan.

Table B-6. Review of NHTSA RD&T Program

Investment Criterion	Program Evidence
Relevance	• Research program is mission-oriented and supports NHTSA and DOT goals.
	• Specific goals and priorities for the next five years are laid out in the *NHTSA Vehicle Safety Rulemaking and Research Priority Plan*.
	• NHTSA's research programs support regulatory actions and other initiatives that prevent thousands of fatalities and serious injuries each year.
	• NHTSA research addresses clearly identified safety problems and seeks new solutions that make maximum use of advanced technologies.
	• Research programs often involve cooperative efforts with foreign governmental agencies, the automotive industry, and other vehicle-safety-related organizations.
Quality	• NHTSA research findings are frequently presented to other NHTSA offices, thus ensuring critical internal review.
	• NHTSA research findings are frequently presented to the public in a variety of formats, ensuring critical outside review.
	• NHTSA research results are presented in international forums and are often the basis of actions taken by international bodies.
	• Investment decisions are based on competition and merit review whenever possible.
Performance	• Key research milestones are identified and tracked in performance targets.
	• The NHTSA research program provides input for cost-benefit studies of alternative solutions to safety problems.

Table B-7. Review of PHMSA RD&T Program*

Investment Criterion	Program Evidence
Relevance	• All RD&T supports DOT's safety strategic objective.
	• Planning workshops held by the Office of Pipeline Safety (OPS) provide stakeholder input on RD&T gaps and priorities.
	• An OPS Blue Ribbon Panel comments on program priorities and performance measures.
Quality	• To the extent possible, PHMSA awards research contracts and grants through a competitive, merit-based process.
	• Retrospective quality review is provided through the OPS Blue Ribbon Panel and customer outreach.
Performance	• The RD&T budget aligns program activities with specific performance goals.
	• The budget identifies sources of data for measuring success or failure in achieving the goals.
	• All goals support broader DOT objectives.
	• RD&T performance is retrospectively documented in DOT's annual *Performance and Accountability Report*.

*PHMSA was part of the former RSPA when this review for FY 2005 was conducted.

Table B-8. Review of RITA RD&T Program*

Investment Criterion	Program Evidence
Relevance	• All activities support Departmental objectives for safety and organizational excellence.
	• The TRB Committee for Review of the National Transportation Science and Technology Strategy oversees and reports on strategic planning activities.
	• A review of the UTC program by George Washington University (GWU) found that all stakeholders surveyed had "extremely favorable" or "somewhat favorable" impressions of the program.
Quality	• RITA awards research contracts and grants through a competitive, merit-based process to the extent possible.
	• Retrospective quality review is provided through the TRB and stakeholder outreach.
Performance	• GWU found that the UTCs are achieving the three core objectives of the program as directed by Congress.
	• The RD&T budget aligns program activities with specific performance goals.
	• The budget identifies sources of data for measuring success or failure in achieving the goals.
	• All goals support broad DOT objectives.
	• Performance is retrospectively documented in DOT's *Performance and Accountability Report*.

*This FY 2005 review addressed the activities of the former RSPA's Office of Innovation, Research, and Education, which are now carried out by the Office of RD&T in RITA.

U.S. Department of Transportation

Research and Innovative Technology Administration

www.ingramcontent.com/pod-product-compliance
Lightning Source LLC
Chambersburg PA
CBHW052014280526

45793CB00005B/981